Two Places

Two Places

Lenore Weiss

Aldrich Press

ISBN-13: 978-0615999609

Cover Art: Leslie Weissman

Kelsay Books
Aldrich Press
24600 Mountain Avenue 35
Hemet, California 92544

For Ilya and Mischa

Contents

First Place

Börte's Perfect Love Song

Börte was the first wife of Temujin (Chinggis Khaan). She was captured by the Merkid tribe and temporarily married to Chilger the Athlete. Chinggis Khaan, known to Western audiences as Genghis Khan, began his drive to unite the clans of the Asiatic steppes in an effort to reclaim her.

1. Börte Sings Both Loudly and Softly to Temujin

I am Mongol, loyal to one master.
When that other khan

touches my cheek, it turns into a salt pond.
Nightmares rim my eyes with darkness.

My husband, Temujin, is a gray wolf
who kissed my mouth.

I remember when Temujin lifted
the fringe of my silk banner

with his spear.
Now his spirit pole is gone from my tent.

I drip candle wax along the fissure of my heart,
drink warm kumis.

A woman in black sable calls me
to stand before my dream.

Floating seeds join each other in air.
I hear them laugh.

The seed in my bowl is not his.
It doubles me.

I will slip away like the whip of a horsetail
upon the frozen steppe.

I was not born to die in another clan's tent.
The Blue Sky follows me between branches.

The face of the marmot and falcon is Temujin's
face. The birch hides my secret.

2. The Lichen Clan

Stolen from Temujin to this mirror camp, days
stick in my throat and sicken me.

I see men, women, and children
with the same two arms and legs.

They stare
and wait for me to circle.

If I remove my silver necklace,
I must bow my neck.

How long can I nurse emptiness,
a heartless child?

The fire at night warms bootless feet.
My silver gelding with a black tail does not run toward me.

I search the Altai Mountains for rising dust.
Before a cooking fire,

I dry a blanket, the same color
as an arrow that strikes

the curved tip of a falcon's wing.
I see it.

Men come to crush each other,
and every woman and child with two arms and legs.

Stallions mash bones with hooves
into the black rock of Lake Baikal

covered with the faces of lichen
that speak as one clan.

3. Wild Onion and Pear

Lying next to this man, Chilger,
through the smoke-hole of our tent,

I hear a grasshopper
burrow in sheep dung.

He throws a hand over my chest
like a lasso pole to draw me in tight.

His breath travels up an elk-path
and comes back down, snorting.

All night, even without sleep,
I cannot rest.

I'm the one who holds his willow branch
until it topples,

and in the morning, the one who fills
a leather bucket with mare's milk

until it runs down his face
and drowns him in a white river.

I draw my lips over my teeth.
He wants to capture a smile.

He can bridle me.
No one commands my heart.

Only the child that floats on its back
with fingers pressed against my belly.

I will dig in the ground,
feed him wild onion and pear.

4. A Wolfskin With a Silk Rope

My ears hear everything at night.
My eyes see everything during day.

I could not tell who entered my tent
through the evening smoke-hole and stood

with his legs, an arrow's width apart.
Then I saw him.

Sky blue. Even his nose.
Maybe he was a cloud.

In his hand, several wolfskins tied
with a silk rope.

He said: *From the water of your waters*
will grow a nation. Four sons

with the strength of a wolf pack
tied together.

He placed a bundle in my lap.
When I awoke, it was my head's soft pillow.

Then I knew Temujin would come.
Who else could be the father of such men?

Part of me
wanted daughters to braid my hair,

to brew tea when news of the tangled grass
reached my ears.

Piles of rotting bodies like dead trees.
I am not prepared.

5. The Strongest Hand

Soldiers drink horse's blood,
fill moats with dead bodies,

pile catapults with excrement
near a thousand flickering fires.

Quivers of horn and wood
hug arrows for their intended.

Ashes of men rout a birch
with locust memories.

Now I pour ashes into my palm
and blow breath on them,

men in a season of slaughter
who disappear beneath a saddle.

When I was a child,
my mother carried me on her hip.

I wore boots as soft as doeskin.
One day she found a mare,

escort to a pool of water
between shoulders of earth.

The sky grew black. I could see back
to the beginning

before I held a horse's mane
and breathed in its sweet sweat,

where I sat and wondered why people kill each other,
and then scatter to the strongest hand.

6. A Sparrow in Search of Spring

Temujin, wolf-man with cat eyes
came to me in a goat-skin cape

to replace my companion of months,
a shadow. Now my twin flies

like a sparrow in search of spring
away to a peak covered in grass,

or like a sturgeon that leaps
with the oar of its tail.

I run free.
Night is studded with pearls

and wraps us in black velvet.
Inside each other's den,

no one sees
what we do,

our backs etched raw
by root and stone.

Thunder from our sated voices
widens a stream-bed.

Who we are together
shines in our eyes.

The child that is mine
becomes his.

Temujin has come back.
I pick out straw from his beard.

The Last Days of Genghis Khan

Forgive me, my sons,
gathered inside this tent
with its smoke hole open to the Great Sky.

I wasn't there to watch your feet
stretch into stirrups, or to guide your arm
as you raised an arrow to bow.

What can I say? I've failed to show
how a Mongol can make a mountain
change places with horses and men.

But even as frost leaches my breath,
I wish to be a father who fills your saddlebag
with the wild onion of my own journey:

how being a leader is to master pride,
more difficult
to quell than a wild lion,

or anger, harder to subdue than the greatest wrestler.
Never think of yourself as the strongest or smartest.
When animals climb to the top of a mountain,

they cast a shadow
along rocks where they stand.
Remember to say only what needs to be said.

A loose mouth leaves crumbs for the wind
to heap upon the plates of your enemy.
Have vision and goals,

easy to throw away once a fast horse
and jeweled women adorn your arm.
Conquering an army

is not the same as conquering a nation.
You conquer an army with tactics and men,
a nation by winning the hearts of its people.

Loyalty to family is what you have as brothers
and the only thing you will ever have
in this smoky world of dreams laced with cinnamon.

Manduhai the Wise

In the Year of the Tiger
when people could not sleep in their tents,

or birds in their nests,
I, Manduhai, Mongolian queen,

did not lift the tent flap of the man
whom people thought to share my bed,

but carried the spirit pole of my ancestors,
Dayan Khan, a cripple whose

bones were massaged with camel's milk
and warmed in a silver bowl. I rescued the boy,

strapped him to my horse in a basket,
raised him on the battlefield

to be Great Khan, heir of Genghis.
Girls threw offerings of milk in the air.

Later when the steppes became mud,
we stepped through mud together,

and when it was cold,
we warmed our hands by the same fire.

With him, my waters gave birth to eight sons
and together we covered Mongolia

with the hooves of our mares.
From the Tuul River to the Orkhon,

we were two shafts of one cart
drawn by a white camel.

And when I could no longer
bear armor,

his memory was silk
on my heart and limbs.

Manduhai Across the Router

On weekends I Skype you,
wash sheets I bought when you lived here,
fall down on the bed.

There's no coffee in the house.
I remember my dream where ribs of darkness
decayed into a sandstorm of light bulbs.

Nothing about coffee.
Fire, glass, and alcohol were part of it.
The Borromeo String Quartet scanned

Handel from laptops on music stands.
The iPhone glowed blue
with our songs.

I pressed Shuffle,
they fell flat.
Technology

a Genghis Khan
shooting from the hip
and the World Wide Web,

a Spice Trail across
routers with worm holes.
Later from the estuary

I emailed memories
scented in lavender, rosemary,
and the back of your neck.

Hazel Nuts and Sour Cherry Juice

Women on the plane wore headscarves, others neck pillows, shoes from all over the mall. The only constant was the omnipresence of cellphones and iPads, clusters of people gathered around recharging stations. If Apple can't make money, who can? Attendants distributed zippered pouches complete with toothpaste, socks, lip balm, and earplugs. It looked like a shoeshine kit. The bathroom contained lemon verbena lotion and cologne. Dark-haired attendants served hazel nuts and sour cherry juice during beverage service. The chef wore a white cap and apron. The Albanian man sitting next to me hugged an Italian suit in his lap throughout the nine and a half hour flight for his upcoming son's wedding in Italy. The plane flew across Canada, Newfoundland, across Ireland, England, France, Germany, Yugoslavia to Istanbul. Look up Charlie Gibbs Fracture Zone. Maury Sea Channel. Rhodope Mountains. Kazablanka spelled like I've never seen it before. Babies getting shushed by their mothers. An eighteen-month old stole my spoon. An adoring grandmother turned to make sure I didn't get ugly. I walked around the Grand Bazaar until my room was ready, visited the Basilica Cistern that was built by Roman Emperor Justinian in the sixth century. A photo crew crowded Medusa's head. There were more people getting their hair done in salons than eating in restaurants. Hawkers attacked me with Chanel perfume, a child's top, and a scarf. I went back to the hotel and checked my cellphone for email.

Get Your Dervish On

The call to prayer resounds five times a day. Calligraphic signature of ancient architects on ebony doors are encrusted with mother of pearl. Turkish is related to Hungarian, the same Ugric-Altaic language stem akin to Finnish, also possibly to Korean and Japanese. Think Mongolian. According to guides, the city is built upon layers of who does not like whom. Green and blue chariot teams once faced off along political lines. Ethnic groups fill out the corners of the city. Think Kurds, Greeks, Armenians. Scratch a civilization. Find a welt. We visited a Whirling Dervish ceremony. Ten dervishes appeared in black gospel-like robes, hands tucked across chests to signify the unity of God. One leader sat on a red sheepskin and kissed each hat as the dervishes bowed. Save for black robes, everything else was white. Off with the black, spin toward the white. The fundamental condition of our existence is to revolve like atoms, something I heard from a yoga teacher. White skirts billowed into human planets of love. The ceremony ended with a prayer for peace. Fade to black.

Hi Dad, It's Me

I visited the Ashkenazi Synagogue near the Galata Tower. On a
street ornamented with cellphones and fans. Everything Electronik.
Went inside a building the color of old stones, the way you looked
lying on a hospital bed. Anyhow, I saw a picture of Moses hugging
the Ten Commandments. Then I realized it was Jesus carrying the
Cross. Good joke, huh? Kemal, a university student selling leather
purses near the Tower, told me he came back from the United
States because his father was dying. Wherever you are, I hope you
are well. You would like the soft red leather here.

Wish You Were Here

Idiot boss man who sat me down two weeks after my husband died and told me how I was a fuckup, I can see your fat face floating in Istanbul's Basilica Cistern before the Tourist Authority cleaned up the place, mouth filled with a salad of rotten tomatoes and cucumber peelings, spaces between your toes, sewers for carp. Around the corner, cameras flash in your eye sockets. Did you know that Roman Emperor Justinian built the Cistern in the sixth century? You always went with the winner. Don't forget, you're scheduled for an appointment with Medusa in her corner office. She's drop dead gorgeous.

Medusa

Medusa, the marketeers paraded you
up and down the red carpet
snapping photographs

to appear the next day on CNN
and Entertainment Tonight,
social media clamoring

for another look at your shocked face
and the hairstyle (the hairstyle!)
Does anyone know

where she came from?
a beach babe Babylon
in the Coliseum

raining down from the upper decks
to the bullpen,
a performance piece

posted on a thousand
Facebook pages. Medusa,
all the stars are trembling trending tonight.

Magic in Istanbul

Sitting here in the Kybele Hotel on the first of August, the first trip I've made across the Atlantic these long years of my life, I didn't know I liked hotel rooms.

The ones I've stayed in had TV sets with black remotes on a nightstand, a breakfast of Cheerios and Froot Loops with containers of too-sweet yogurt and a piece of plastic to open the door with a swipe, which is no way to enter a room. It's how a thief enters a room.

A door must be opened with anticipation. A door leads somewhere.

A door must be closed the same way, the way I learned to end my marriage and to walk into your arms that evening.

Here I have a brass key attached to something that looks like a lipstick tube.

I didn't realize how I loved being away from home, not the weekend jaunt to Calistoga or driving to Monterey to smell an iodine haze with miles of shoreline fringed in kelp, really being away and tasting white peaks of yogurt, smelling fish being grilled on the Galata Bridge, hearing language and only being able to guess at its meaning.

I didn't know how much I missed conversation over velvety cups of Turkish coffee.

Conversation takes time. There is all the time in the world here, minarets dripped from an architect's hand to make the sky ache with envy.

I didn't realize how much I loved wandering down streets and making them my own, hearing men call me, "Madame."

I didn't know I would love the Imam's call to prayer, a five points bulletin from every mosque in Istanbul. The prayer makes me change lanes away from the world of buying and selling.

In that prayer, I hear the echo of a cantor singing on Yom Kippur, the harmonies of Gregorian Chants, throat singing of Mongolian priests. The sound finds a deep burrow where it scrabbles forward and blinks at the sun.

But constantly? I've never loved anyone telling me what to do.

I know the black dress, tunics, and headscarves are meant to ward off defilement. My Turkish sisters tell me from beneath the Roman arch of their eyebrows, they are moving at their own pace, in their own time. They tell me I can't understand. I don't understand.

I didn't realize how much I loved hearing your voice on the telephone in Room 404 of the Kybele Hotel where lanterns glow with magic, and how much I wanted to touch you again.

In Istanbul, Poem for Wednesday

Too many stores spilling over with fans on hot days, too many
water bottles abandoned at the bottom of trees near small children,
too many brass lanterns that demand more magic in a world run by
computers, too many people who have lost their lanterns, too many
marble staircases slick with rain, too many burned-out houses and
sunken windows.

I feel tired from a dream about my mouth
being gagged with a black scarf.
I feel thirsty for coffee with velvet at the bottom of my cup.
I feel curious to know if Nazim Hikmet's Türkeye still lives.
I know Orhan Pamuk's is before me.

Too many minarets of Turkish Delight tiled in pastel colors,
mulberry roll-ups from trees that used to be a one-stop shop for
silk worms, too many cats, skinny, dirty, lounging in the center of
storefront bowls to bring in business, too many extra tram tickets
and no Turkish Lira, too many umlauts crowding letters like black
eyes staring everywhere.

I feel I may need a smaller purse.
I feel ready to peel off my sweaty clothes
in the Hippodrome fountain.
I feel a longing to get a new cat.

Too many red carpets, too many security guards bored by standing
at the crossroads of civilization, too many boxes encrusted with
mother-of-pearl petals crowding other mother-of-pearl petals on
every other box, too many motor bikes that have lost their brakes,
too many kebabs that make me feel sorry for lambs, too many
bounty hunters for credit cards.

I feel ready to fly with a bird that never looks down,
I feel scared to unpack wings from my knapsack.
I feel confused.

Too many ways to spend money, too many layers black and scabby
plastered into the rat hole of history, too many unshelled pistachios
that point fingers, too many calls on Skype that don't get through,
too many prayers that go unanswered.

I feel amazed by a silver dragonfly on a girl's earlobe.
I feel wonder at the arched Roman column
         of the same girl's eyebrow.
I find joy in every pair of eyes walking along
         these cobblestone streets.

In Istanbul: Faith Has No Name

1
Old men talking on park benches
sound the same in every country,
a soft humming of the same tune,

witnesses to toppled governments,
news of sickness, grinding bad business
or help extended from a distant relative.

Some old men sit and read a book,
a single finger holds their place.

2
Today it's about a cat that stalks a pigeon.
I sit in a cafe and drink Turkish coffee.
A woman balances breakfast on her knees.

I pass through three security gates,
climb two sets of stairs,
enter the women's section of the Sephardic Temple.

The song of the cantor leaves a fragrance in the air,
an incense of belief travels on the sob of gulls.

3
I leave tomorrow.

I will not hear the call of the Imam on the last day of Ramadan.
The Internet will inform me of more bombings and killings.

I want to ask why faith must be named.
Why belief must be branded. Why Arabic and Hebrew
can't walk down the same street together?

Faith is an arch protecting the weirs of our minds.

It's my own voice talking to myself.

—For Vefa and the staff of the Kybele Hotel

Body Scrubber of the Bath House

Ottoman Dome curved above our wet bodies,
the first time I saw you,
your breasts hung naked,
two gunny sack badges
from nursing children and men's sorrows.
You wore them proudly, offered me directions.

Lady. There. Go. 10 minutes.

I was stretched on a red towel.
my back pressed against the milky marble.

You told me your Turkish name meant flower or happy,
and turned your face away as if you were not telling the truth.

Then you started to work me over,
tossed brass bowls of lukewarm water down my back,
over my head, scrubbed me hard from the heat, my sweat,
let me feel shreds of my dead skin,
washed me like my mother.

You were not afraid to touch the scar
running down the middle of my belly,

scrubbed behind my ears, slapped my back,
eased my body between your thighs and held me there, wet.
I found your cave of warmth and leaned into it.
I was your baby. You could've done anything to me.

Lady. You go. There.

I crawled on my stomach, face down,
breathed marble, steam, dome
cupped against my back.
I was a specimen butterfly pinned to your lap.

Then the body scrubber of the bath house, sang,
notes curved in the air,
calligraphy from an empire
and its attendant women.

Everything went black.

Prayer for My Daughter

May you always find cochineal insects
to anoint your cheeks bright red
in holiday parades marching down Broadway,
a dozen balloon floats
tugging after you and repeating,
"Here she comes,
the clown of parapomegranatism."

May you always carry a vanilla bean
to taste on your lips
even when you have lost faith
in para-
pomegranatism
and the sun forgets to rise in the east,
blood pumping through cloud banks
to light the way of doves.

All this I wish for you,
breath of my breath,
seed of my seed,
the red pomegranate spiral,
the one for whom I cut open
the sweet fruit.

Daughter's GPS Device

You've left your husband for the third time.
Tell yourself this time you really mean it.
Recall how I used to twist
my marriage band around my finger.
Or maybe it's nothing like that at all.

Maybe you're nine months pregnant and feel a contraction,
make the mistake of calling my old number.
At the next Stop sign, you grab something in the car
that sticks to your finger like batter to fried chicken
when you moan, *Oh*.

Or maybe this week you're driving the kids to their soccer game.
You're lost, turn on the GPS.
November is butting up against the holidays. You remember
the macaroni and cheese our family ate one year
and how you still can't get yours to taste like mine.

Which is when I come in,
a visit from a far-away place
where sparrows dip every morning
into a jar of night.

Open my mouth to tell you I'm here, I'm here.
Run my voice across your thick hair.
Now it's my turn to miss you.

Bayou Bartholomew

Maybe it took Istanbul
to get me here in one piece
here in your place on Eastlake Road
where Bayou Bartholomew is filled with tree trunks
sticking out from the mud
like the end of frizzed out mop handles
sneaking up on a bucket of water.

Maybe I wasn't sure it was worth the risk,
even if it were, the odds of anything happening,
so teensy-weensy, it would've been a waste.

Maybe I needed to convince myself
the way Indiana Jones
rescued a dying Sean Connery
by leaping across an illusion.

I am procrastinating, part of the foreplay
of the little red, tangle and hard
singing a song that taxes the air with gulps,
a place we went to so easily,
a Bronx girl who grew up mining
the museums of New York City
and you, a boy from cotton farms
who grew up on a bus playing country.

Maybe it took going to Istanbul to get here,
bungee jumping from the top of a mosque
and riding the rain to the edge of myself.
I stood there and saw you.

Plane Time

I dreamed a silicon chip looked like an Aztec mask,
a great yawning blackness where a mouth should be.

A dying vampire awoke in a pool of perspiring blood
cared for by a young woman with a baby.

A Dallas waveform appeared.
Bachman Lake, sun sparks on oil floating?

The flight is filled with ruby, gold, and platinum passengers.
Overhead bins are closed to inquiry.

Red safety cards are hidden in seat pockets.
A bearded lady walks down the aisle.

God's Knock Knock Joke

Some kind of a joke,
to allow me to find love
half-way across the country.
His arms? His lips?
Give me a break. On Skype?

For years I waited for someone
until my room grew dark.
Any silk clothes
I shoved to the back
of my closet.

Maybe you're getting
a kick out of this.
I'm tired of acceptance.
I want to press my skin
against his sweet breath,

not walk in the door
to a blinking message machine.
Did I say how his hair
is the color of spring
on wet pavement,

how his smile lifts me
like the song of a chorus?
I hope you're enjoying this,
to see me hanging
from one side of the bed.

Two Places

Louisiana, home of a thousand Family Dollar stores
and cotton farms planted with corn for ethanol
I think of you as I return to Oakland,

report for jury duty with hundreds
of others waiting to be screened for weapons,
swiping smart phones as if they could save us.

Louisiana, camouflaged in brown leaves
on a breast pocket of lottery tickets and cigarettes.
Another weekend I drive across the Bay Bridge,

pass a coral reef that covers the hills of San Francisco
in window panes of white waves,
I'm lost in a place between two places

where fresh produce arrives from Walmart
and everyone is a po'boy at the gas station.
Louisiana, my hand shimmers in your bayou,

in the Ouachita River where grandmothers
tell stories from a mound of earth,
a bay and a cypress

and the word *hosanna*,
how they grew apart in a well of water.
Louisiana we live in two places.

Second Place

Yahrzeit Candle

Every Sunday you took the subway to the beach,
staked a claim for our blanket near the water.
Back and forth you walked along the shore
wondering why a man had to work six days a week.

But really, you could've been thinking
about a hundred other things—
Money. Bills. Plaster casts cooling like pies.
I can't be sure. For a big man, you left a small footprint.

In your hands immigrants bonded together,
members of a Hungarian-American social club,
in pyramids and arabesques they balanced on your shoulders.
You were the Atlas who held everyone up.

If you weren't at the beach, you made orthopedic shoes
near Second Avenue, now divided between a tarot reader
and a pet grooming shop, a painted Dalmatian
wearing a red, white, and blue hat.

Space shoes they called them back then,
brown and black leather hulks with air holes
so the foot could breathe, you said,
soaking arches in the still waters of acetone.

But what reminds me of you more than the two packs of Marlboros
you smoked every day for years before your first operation,
the glue you used to join leather to a metal backing,
so strong, its smell bullied a pathway to the lungs.

Over the years, your glue pot cooled and formed its own container
transforming your brush into something beyond a brush,
bristles splayed and petrified in stone salute.
On hands and knees, far from the low tides

of Long Island Sound, I embalm tiles for a slate backing
with the same stuff that sticks to my gloves,
here on the anniversary of your death
thinking about you these forty-three years gone,

each stroke, a burning.

—for my father, Martin Weiss

Note: A Yahrzeit (Yiddish for "a year's time") marks the anniversary of a loved
one's death. The candle burns for twenty-four hours, and is lit on the date of that
person's death.

Hands and Feet

Large hands my father had,
nails bruised
purple and clipped jagged
from a buffing machine
disguised in his shop
as a sleeping child,
until he stood up to the thing,
pressed an iron pedal
and caused the breath of the beast
to heave in bright sparks
and whine inconsolably
sanding arches
into a slalom course for feet.

He always caught my hand
by two fingers
at Pelham Bay Parkway
the last stop
on the subway
we waited for a bus
to drop us off
at the bath house
where the floor
was cold and gritty
without shoes
looked for an occasional penny
to turn up on a wash of sand,
back and forth
he schooled me in complexity:
the foot is a delicate instrument, he said,
composed of more bones
than any other part of the body,

(28 if you included those at the base
of the big toe, 26 if you didn't).

He mixed a white frosting
from Plaster of Paris,
shaped shoes
to his customer's bunions,
fallen arches,
a fractured metatarsal
allowing feet
to walk without pain,
allowing me to hold his hand
on a Sunday afternoon
and look up at the blue sky.

Letter to My Mother

I knew I wasn't going to make it,
driving past rows of palm trees in the taxi
mourning the heat from 400 feet up in the Miami summer
while you'd dehydrated on the trip down
from the 24th floor of Co-op City in the Bronx
and died before I could touch your hand.
Not exactly the kind of vacation you had planned.

Daddy had died a year before
in another hospital where the ceiling flaked.

You couldn't admit he was on his way out,
made all of us, your daughters swear
we would zip up our mouths.

When I was younger, I wanted to scream
until my throat collapsed—
for your not allowing
me to say good-bye to my father.
Maybe I should've blamed myself for listening.

Anyhow, that's a bed-time story for sleepwalkers,
almost forty years after your last dream
of diving from a rockweed-covered pier,
sea bladders filled with air pops
that you sucked for the first three miles
until you exhausted yourself
and were pulled down down
into the witch's lair.

You were the first one who taught me
how to swim
placed your hands
beneath my stomach and told me to kick,
not to be afraid, you would always hold me.
But I knew when you'd let go.

You caught me then, beneath my belly,
a guppy you brought home
from Woolworth's one afternoon in a plastic bag
filled with water, you joked how my sisters
had been rescued from a garbage can, strong stock
from the beer halls of Budapest to places
where violets grew like gourds
whose purples I've never seen.

Be there, and I would try to find you on the street,
in the high Magyar cheekbones of a woman
waiting to order her half a pound of rye sliced without seeds,
I would attack any stranger with my hands
and hug her knees.

Whippoorwill

I looked everywhere for you riding the down escalator
on my way to the bargain table at Alexander's
where you took me to find a dress
in a girl's 10 Chubby—but I'm no longer that size.

I wanted to find you at the Automat on 14th street
near the macaroni and cheese where you showed me
how to open a window by inserting a quarter,
plates of food on white dishes fit for a Queen.

Bedtime you recited The Song of Hiawatha,
By the shores of Gitchee Gumee, by the shining Big-Sea-Water.
Fog rolled across my bed and whippoorwills
preened their feathers, called to each other to come home.

I lost you at the Museum of Natural History
standing behind the guard rail of the Tyrannosaurus Rex,
each rib as tall as an apartment building
ready to collapse on my head.

On baking day, your yeast cakes rose in our bed,
silky beneath tenement covers, until they grew
and doubled in size beneath your hands
dusted with flour. I did. I tried to find you.

Mahalo to Mom in Kaua'i

Drive the rental far from chain-linked traffic
to bamboo forests shielded in philodendron
and up the basalt side of mountains
where everything is endangered and hidden

where Menehune farmed taro
and built fish-pond walls.

Later came the plantation workers
eating rice from tin pots in the fields.
Chinese, Japanese, Filipino, Korean,
Portuguese, Puerto Rican.

Mahalo, I walk along the beach,
can almost feel my mother's fingers
wrapped around my hand,
me, a young girl tracing our walk in wet sand.

Now with all the helicopters in the sky
you'd think this was Oakland,
every forty minutes a new tour flies
over the Na Pali coast,
a pilot points to a beach where Nellie
in *South Pacific* washed a man
right out of her hair.

In the morning, I'd rubbed myself
with sun block in front of the television,
a news anchor interviewed a man who demonstrated
how to make *poi* the old way, pounding the root and rolling it
between his fingers.
Good, the host pronounced. *Very good.*

I've been laid off, a family to support—
Your voice churns in the undertow—
tribes have always migrated
to a fresh watering hole.

Palm trees rub fronds and blow apart.

Note: Mahalo is the Hawaiian word for thank you, gratitude, admiration, praise or esteem.

Sisters

For years I didn't like either one of you,
felt I was returning the favor—
the baby, an annoyance, an inconvenience,
the one you dragged on the subway to go ice-skating,
left me holding the railing.

In a one-bedroom apartment, slept
on a twin bed in the corner of the room,
got up early on Saturday while you both snoozed,
turned on the TV low in the living room,
our parents heaped in snores and covers.

We tied scarves to our wrists,
pop beads hung from our necks,
danced in front of the dresser mirror,
Bronx gypsies who sniffed
a forest from a cedar box.

Sometimes I watched
sparrows leap across the slats of a fire escape,
played in the Bryant Avenue lot
strained mica from sandstone on rusted screens
into soup cans, counted chicory
stalks and dandelions, climbed the ditch
to Lafayette Avenue and walked back again.

You both seemed so far away—
growing up and getting married,
a shadow play of choices on a wall outside of me.

Dickens' Christmas Carol,
the ghost of things to come,
but if I reformed my Scrooge—
what I saw didn't have to be.

2.
Sometimes in front of the moon
of a satellite dish I ask the waves
to cast me back, before they left so early,
our parents who live in a framed photograph.

Joined a generation,
healed myself in California
beneath redwood trees and tide pools
and manzanita

calling out *sister, sister,*
to see if I could hear you
from the other side of the Old World.

You rolled inside a barrel of work
and family and lived in a different time-zone,
waited for me to come to my senses.

I found my own epoch.
It took years.

3.
Driving back home from Baton Rouge
I pass egrets of plastic bags caught in grass,
houses tottering on stacks of red bricks,
windows with blackened eye lids.

Leveled by wrinkles,
we are close in age now,
no longer the beauties
of Orchard Beach doing birdies

in the air with our father
who held us there
until we found our own blue sky.

A Person of Carriage

"They are gone, the pepper trees,
the tiny buds of phosphorus."
—*Federico Garcia Lorca*

She spoke with a Hungarian accent, her speech
bordered on vines and blue forget-me-nots
dropped her w's in soft cushions beneath my feet,
took a bowl of oatmeal for breakfast with cottage cheese.
Mid-morning she drank orange pekoe tea in a glass,
prunes and pears spiked with cloves,
anointed herself in the mirror with 4711 cologne.

She knew what she liked and I liked everything she did,
walked with her head held high, a person of carriage
who twisted her chestnut hair into a chignon
caught with a tortoise shell or silver comb.
She bought fabric to create her own clothes,
nubs of wool—purple, rust, and forest green,
an oil landscape lined in pure silk.

She painted her canvases wearing overalls,
but not on Shabbos when she folded
a napkin on her head,
paper peaks making her look stylish,
singing evening prayers along the tops
of burning candles whose lights she gathered
along the oaken leaf of a table.

She stored her paintings in the back of Uncle Harry's
Brooklyn shoe shop and took us to see her studio,
brushes listing in glass jars like spent soldiers,
the smell of oil paint and charcoal that coated
her nails in a fine dust. I remember how she held
a stick of charcoal between two fingers,
drew to the edge of a paper and stopped.

But mostly, I see her sitting on a rock
near Dudley Pond Farm,
our refuge from the Bronx summer,
her breasts released to the open air
and into her palms like two doves
rescued from the afternoon heat—
she gathered her breasts to her mouth,
and kissed the pointed tip of each one.

Mameleh

I can still remember what it was like to be
An immigrant without a clock radio
Who knew nothing of the color fuchsia,
In my black shawl between two wait states
Of bread and no bread.
I had no digital pastel cube
From which I volunteered
The morning news to actually wake me up?
What I had, *mameleh*, a music box constructed by
The Watchman himself, a ballerina with a gold foil rose
Tucked behind each ear, a starched skirt made of such lace
You'd only find in a hope chest.
And as she danced around her trolley track–
Poor thing! We both expected so much.

Note: Mameleh is an affectionate Yiddish term for addressing a little girl.

Jochebed

Call me Jochebed, covered with thorns,
The one who burns but is not consumed.
On either side of him, I place a favorite toy.
Maybe he'll come back to play.

I was in night school typing at my desk
When my eldest decided to run a bath for the baby.
He went to the refrigerator and forgot.
I thought it would be okay to leave them.
Nine years old is so much older than seven months.

He called me and cried, "The baby can't be dead."
Floating in a basket of papyrus reeds
Daubed with bitumen and pitch.

Call me Jochebed, covered with thorns,
The one who burns but is not consumed.
I wash the face of my eldest
With hyssop dipped in the basin of my tears.

Note: Jochebed is the name of Moses' birth mother.

Music Box Ballerina on a Low Battery

I told 'em, go for jugular meaning and use open source
as I cut and pasted myself into his picture,
but you didn't want to hold hands in the desert
made everything more complicated.

I tried to explain, how it wasn't my choice
pointed my toe like a hound in heat
when I heard a voice paging someone
for a defibrillator. Fuck. Even G-d's gone high-tech.

My partner in circles,
I can tell you what the media won't say.
An army of poor *shnooks*
cast a giant shadow in sage paint.

Brother, lest you believe in stones
don't throw them at me.
This I keep pirouetting around and around
finding no place
for partial measures, interim agreements,
or road maps leading nowhere.

Note: Shnook is a Yiddish term for a person who is a "Sad Sack" personality;
pitiable, but not despised.

J'Accuse

Amir.
ID card number
12300056712

my biometrics;

hair: brown
eye color: brown
my thumb print: regular like me.

The Tel Aviv District Court blocked me from justice.
Amit Biram, registrar at the Tel Aviv District court,
disrupted legal proceedings.

I suffered a stroke and was granted 100 percent work disability.
Two Ministry of Housing committees rejected my case.

Ask the manager of Aharanov on Shaddai Street.
He knows my story.

I blame the Prime Minister, Bibi Netanyahu
and Minister of Finance, Yuval Steinitz.

I blame the National Health Insurance system,
Ben David, manager of order execution,
and manager of the claims department in Tel Aviv

who seized my truck work equipment.
Is a man supposed to live in a shopping cart?

I blame the Haifa National Insurance branch
who abused me for a year until I got my disability.

I have no money for medicine or rent.
I've paid taxes, served in the army.

Let them call me a deviant.
Let them report I'm a crank.
Let them say my mother licks the hands of Palestinians.

I will not run in the street like a dog for hand-outs.
I am an Israeli citizen.
I want to be treated like a human being.

Note: Based on a letter by an Israeli Jew, Moshe Silman, who became a cab
driver and suffered a stroke that left him unemployed. Silman set himself on fire
in Tel Aviv in July 2012, and before doing so, distributed a letter to the crowd
about the reasons for his action.

The Fool

I recognized my car in the parking lot,
how the rear window is spotted from the past.
To pass time I read the fine print of oysters,
watch out for pyramid schemes.

Once I got lost trying to acquire
kitty litter in Walmart.
It took two days and night vision
to get out of that maze. Amazing.

I never buy what I can hold.
The other day I wanted to do something fun.
I wore a bicycle helmet on an airplane.
A little girl laughed.

Double-Take

Caterpillars hang on branches in a breach of profit.
Catfish and brim float on water, the lake's prophets.

First to pre-board, a man in a wheelchair avoids a hassle.
A man dashes out of the bathroom and forgets his asshole.

A rotisserie of fire ants dig dark carnal knowledge.
Spring laminates brown hills in carnival knowledge.

Exploding pomegranates splatter the earth with a red present.
Corn crops, spears of brown fields provide ethanol a presence.

A water blister of brass and silk opens a time lapse.
Shredded tires along a flooded street do backward laps.

A chocolate bar tattooed on his chest comes á la carte.
A computer is the first place to look for the Holocaust.

Leona Canyon

Sparrows call above the creek's ripple, five-finger ferns are brown stumps barely digitized, water is running as California poppies lean in gangs of orange. The stream with its long tongue tastes stone and wood, an echo of storms plunders the creek, fern fronds are curled up babies ready to unfold into noise. What is dead and what has survived the winter, tree branches rubbed down with a mustard of lichen, blackberry vines already wild. Everything is green and fear dissolves in water with a cold, bitter taste.

The Widow Discovers the Secret
of Leona Canyon

Before dog-walkers with squadrons of panting beasts.
pull up in SUVs, I arrive early—a woman without a pooch
who can be trusted to make a game of counting packets of shit

set aside for some doggie walker's return trip.
I start early, knot a hoodie around my waist,
hiking in the sun I want to lose myself,

balance on a branch of a buckeye tree
with its candelabra of mock lilacs,
walk past hemlock that lace the trail,

everything is a blaze of white
as spring marries summer and loosens her veil.
I dip my hands in water and wash my face.

Anna's hummingbird, with her red crown and red
spotted throat, sips right along with me. Shepherds
follow their off-leash flock up the canyon.

Eastern Tiger Swallowtail

"Coincidences of pattern is one of the wonders of nature."
—*Vladimir Nabokov*

The same evening he plugged himself
into an amplifier and lit up
with the neon of his young manhood,
there, all the time in the background,

as she searched for a place to rest
with the pressure of metamorphosis
knocking her out cold on the concrete patio
making it difficult in the next few weeks
to wash her hair or sit up straight

reading how Nabokov had snuffed
out the life of a silver-studded
butterfly and smelled the vanilla and musk
perfume of its wings on his fingertips.

She got better. He continued to play.
A bass guitar streamed from his fingers
smelling of her hair as he dug a hole
in the backyard where a spider plant revolved
around its own hook.

She went to sleep and bathed herself,
an infant child in the dim light of a dream,
knew it was her by the startled look.

The next morning an Eastern Tiger Swallowtail
outside the garage with black wings and a blue band
sampled Hosta for hours and wouldn't go away.

A Piers Plowman

Traffic grows heavy
as days thin to a core.
A candidate promises
she'll do everything except change history—
I sit in front of a computer

dressed in a nightgown of reversible darkness
that slides across my shoulder,
watch you sweat pixels
transported across a browser,
reassembled on my home page.

Listen to pine needles stir the morning,
see fog outline the coast—
still no state budget.
Emptiness catches me by the hand.
Canada geese plow trees overhead.

Lilac, periwinkle, and violet
with shades of ash. I stare
at cactus on the patio—
color shifts from green
to a crinoline.

Outside I hear a cathedral
gone mad, bangles
on a woman's skull
like a torn shopping bag
stuffed with a mall.

Bring! Bring! Bring! Bring! Bring!

WFH

Working from home and raising children,
my brain and hands connect across a keyboard.
Everything else recedes into the background:
a ring tone, a teakettle, a leaf blower outside my window.
Focus on the problem. Not the error.

Somewhere I hear a boy eating a kernel of popcorn on a first-floor
landing.

A young girl walks by with an iPod strapped to her upper arm and
a Raiders patch on her jeans.

I like how my hands and my brain need each other.

In Israel, the color of a yarmulke is a code
about where a person stands along that country's
divided political line.

On the pond at Leona Canyon,
male and female mallards
survey cattails.

Shabbos Song

Your lips move toward me.
I smell fresh air as it tunnels inside your ear.

I am a lupine that grows behind our apartment,
a trellis of seed pods with a few purple blossoms

at the bottom of my stalk where
you bend to pet them

my body dissolves
in wet wool covered with pine

needles escape through my mouth
so naked, you sniff my den.

Xbox Marks the Spot

The day after Thanksgiving
I'll walk across the Great Mall,

use a credit card with a revolving account
turning pennies into gold and gold into health plans,

living at the edge of a culvert
where security systems cook dinners for the homeless,

taller than I ever thought possible, slinky,
my thighs like Sonya Blade in Mortal Kombat,

a member of my own Special Forces unit,
a knapsack of turkey bones wrapped in tinfoil—

Oh them bones, them precious bones
grow apartments from pizza crust.

I rub a mezuzah on the side of my computer,
conjure up Stephen Hawking on a good day

who stands at midnight in the Garden of Eden

wondering

what God was doing before he broke out the world.

Yom Kippur 2005, Yizkor (Memorial Service)

There's a thumbnail
discarded on the floor

rolling into cat hair,
a tissue blown
into a tent of good-bye kisses.

The nail is
painted glow-in-the-dark and still pink,
reflects light, takes a curtain call. Gone.

I follow the Yiskor
meditation, my thoughts
wander to my new vibrator,

a molded purple plastic
water-proof super glide,
waiting for me at home

tucked between socks and panties
purchased the weekend before
while doing food shopping and going

for a walk with my friend and her dog,
the solemnity of making our days count.

I bless Ace Hardware for Double A
batteries, enter the High Holydays in a blaze.

Goat

Starched white suit, he wears
an olive oil can crown on his head,
carries challah as a scepter,
    a scepter

mixes seeds blown from a thistle
rubbed on the honey sac of a bee
that leans toward Jerusalem,
    Jerusalem

where pebbles rotate in a circle,
strained rusted keys buried
in a mound,
    a mound of salt

near a West Bank settlement,
a pail with yogurt from milk
of a black goat,
    a goat's

milk measured in a silver thimble
mixed in a cup with a broken rim
painted with a yellow asphodel,
    asphodel

of memory dipped in straw
beneath a twist of barbed wire
recorded in the crease of an eye,
    watching

inside the vessel of shimmering heat,
an Angel of Death rises from the desert
where the slaughter goes on and on
    and on.

Note: "Goat" is loosely based on *Chad Gadya* or "One Little Goat"
frequently sung to children during the Passover holiday
commemorating the Exodus from Egypt.

Gossip

About a poetry coordinator sitting beneath an umbrella
who reports so and so
is booking readings all over town
now that she's screwing you know who.

About an editor who thinks she's single
because her husband has gone
on a business trip to Italy for two weeks
while she stays home with her son.

About a manager cut and pasting grants
for a million dollar project into a Word document
who's pissed his boss doesn't know
the first thing about leadership.

About the head of armed forces in Falluja
who said Abu Ghraib happened
because an enlistee tucked his brains
inside a black hood.

About Israelis in the government
who said Palestinians are terrorists
who should go back to where they came from
or get pushed into the sea.

About Palestinians who said Israelis
see history with one eye
don't understand how a tree can die
standing cut down.

In the Shadow of the Middle East

A Spare the Air Day
when public transit
offered free rides
on the house
the ferry fuller
than it'd ever been
caps turned backward
orange hair braids
digital cameras snapping
waves mixed with exhaust
on the hottest day of the year
so packed to the gills
we tipped backward
and water-skied
across the Bay,
but once we passed
beneath the shadow of the bridge,
there we were
on the other side
of something we didn't know yet.

Terrorist Morning Montage

Pre-alarm, she runs in the snow wearing sandals,

when a boom box breathes its bass in the street,
a headline on her porch asks:

Do you need parental permission to fight in a jihad?

Now she's out of bed, TV's on, commercial break.

No-name chickens compete with Foster Farms
to be first on the slaughter block.

She packs lunch, takes a shower, a hip hopera
bouncing to work,

while outside the kitchen window
a red plum tree is half-dead,

except for a single branch
the neighbors didn't saw off for a ladder.

In the bedroom, her husband lances
his finger for blood-sugar levels. High.

Past time ticks
wrinkles skin in goose bumps.

Next comes
croissants, warm milk for breakfast.

Ready to leave, she sets
the house alarm to Explode.

Day of Awe

She excuses herself for cutting me off
in the parking lot; a man holds the door open
as I leave the bakery balancing a coffee and a roll.

Maybe it takes terrorism
plus an impending war
to be pleasant.

Tract homes wind around clumps of oak.
The shadow of a bird dips.
A hawk.

Caught in the crossfire between cigarette
cigar smoke just to be near other people,
I sit on a wooden bench, wait for my friend.

We are spending money
in these days
before a massive U.S. strike.

I am one small person
who believes there must be another way,
not a sequel to a World War II movie

no one cares to watch.
Crazy.
I change my seat.

Ben Jonson Makes a Visual Display—Haibun

Macy's is brightly wrapped inside electronic wreaths. Shoppers use umbrellas to duel with rain as I, and 650 other lucky people, crammed inside the basement of the Grand Hyatt, two escalators down. We'd come to hear Edward Tufte, an information architect par excellence who teaches "by the book," that is, by all his remarkable books, sharing case studies, visuals, analysis, and scholarship.

He brought along his personal 430 year-old copy of Euclid's Geometry signed by Ben Jonson. *The Fox.* An assistant thumbed through pages wearing latex gloves. Only if I had been sitting aisle side so I could've seen the poet's signature. Instead, I listened to Tufte talk about how bulleted lists excise richness from thought, how our small screen world is making us stupid.

Since I spend most of my time in front of one of these devices, what will this make me in the next 10 years? I can't wait to spend time with his gorgeous books and keep the man talking inside my ear to help ward off inevitable idiocy.

Oh, for a heavy ceramic cup of tea.

on the surface
of the steel-and-glass table
Euclid's Geometry

How I Went to Jail

"To study the history of mentalities is to enter the arena of human experience most resistant to change."
—*Marc Bloch, The Historian's Craft*

You have to be aware of cultural differences, if marketing wants to insert periods after each letter of UK, or if the German store wants to translate into either high or low, and whether the Japanese approve of a wayward Kanji character. I start with English.

Driving to work I watch clouds cast shadows over the foothills, the hide of a prehistoric animal. Light moves closer to autumn.

Past the mall towers of Hayward and Fremont I drive with a nail in my tire. There's the old Nummi plant now transmogrified into Tesla, an electric car manufacturer; Solyndra, a half a million dollars to be a bright star.

But what's that I hear? KZSU, companion of these fifty minute rides down to Cupertino where the deejay is having broadcast problems because she's doing homework at the same time she's doing her show.

See white rabbit enter building through rear security gate and swipe employee ID. Green. Down an orange hallway, engineers run with laptops.

Soon I find my way to Lake Tahoe, which isn't Lake Tahoe, but Great Salt Lake, all conference rooms are named after lakes. I was invited to sit around the table with helpings of stale pretzels and fudge cookies to thrash out the next business requirements document. An entire wall covered in arrows and boxes—petroglyphs from a high-tech era.

I got my first café latte this evening and it was good. Then I toured
noticed a defibrillator cabinet installed outside
the bathroom where toilets have two flushing options—
manual and automatic.

Time is tied to the device. There are no clocks. I walk softly and
try not to look like an idiot.

Ask not for whom the grass blower whines. This morning it's time
for coffee with a dose of Dr. Oz, maybe Jewelry TV with a siren
call of tanzanite and mocha diamonds. I put the program on mute.
Odysseus was on to something. Boot up the computer on my living
room table layered with a history of Genghis Khan whose armies
made no technological breakthroughs, passed skills through
mountains.

I'm having an out-of-cart body experience. Jewelry TV says
there's only 60 more seconds left on the tanzanite cross.

Genghis Khan had assembled representatives from the world's
religions for a theological bake-off. No side was able to convince
the other of anything.

Christians started to sing. Muslims responded by reciting
the Koran; Buddhists retreated into meditation. Jews did nothing
because it was Shabbos. Instead, everyone got drunk together.

The BBC announced that Americans will boot the economy on
Black Friday, cheerleaders dressed in jogging suits filling shopping
carts. There are no baskets at Walmart, only carts.

I stand near a shelf stocked with every kind of thing for holiday shoppers—pineapple rings, cranberries, chicken broth, baking powder and tins of cinnamon. Standing room only for mincemeat and bags of marshmallows.

I lock-up stuff behind bars and bail them out
at the check-out counter.

I'll do time later.

Seven Things I Will Not Think About in the Last Seconds of My Life

I will not think about my retirement account. I will rest inside a concession stand of white gauze, sun hot. I will ask for water loaded with chunks of ice as a pinball machine rises from Poseidon's eyebrow. I swallow chrome balls like egg yolks slipped into a swimming pool of cake batter. Lights flash. The machine will tilt. Or maybe it will be cold and drizzly.

I will not think about being late for zumba and the hip-hop music that sings over the speakers about my *Sexy Body*. I move my toe to the rhythm of the kitchen clock and realize it speaks Swahili. Each tick repeats a sound: *marehemu, marehemu*. Felix the Cat stands at the center of the kitchen clock with hands outstretched for donations.

I will not think if my heels are rough against my bedcovers, nor will I be bothered by callouses or bunions that stick out like unwanted children. Instead, I will stare at the tattoo on the base of my foot; remember what transpired as I lay on a padded table surrounded by ink roses that climbed higher than I could ever dream.

I will not think if I need to go shopping. I will never need to visit the squat aisles of desire again. What I want is to move my thigh against your thigh, and then my left leg, and then my right leg. Water meanders down my spine. A flight of white pigeons thunders across my mind.

I will no longer think about remembering my passwords or where they are stored, lost the abracadabra consisting of eight digits, a combination of numbers and letters, upper and lower case and containing one symbol. I want an ampersand. I have lost my vowels. No more unique passwords except for a skeleton key that opens all passageways in a shudder of shoes.

I will not think if I can do the electric slide.

I will not think about dying.

American Dream Sequence

It was a humzinger of a dream, baby, I dreamed it for you, baby. Gypsy Rose Lee put away your feathers. Things get muddled with interlocking conglomerates high profit on the margin kind of dreams my mother wanted me to be a teacher not a stripper take the summer off with my husband and kids my dream more like book shelves and fern bars, the gypsy rose lee syndrome arrears again maybe there's more depression than meets my dream boat walking through the dining room to the refrigerator for a cold beer something Victorian with velvet on a mountain top. Martin dreamed his dream for all dreamers didn't book a non-refundable flight knew what ran beneath those streets paved with gold.

Blood money drips with tears and Quentin Tarantino movies exploding myths bodies convulsing until the last man is standing always a last man or a best man or a first man Adam pressing a buzzer to choose the Voice. Question fielded to the audience: What does everyone have, but few can realize? A dream to be or not to be Golde from *Fiddler on the Roof* lighting candles on a white tablecloth so all in the family will holla back with news of winning the lottery paying off credit cards sending kids to college in the olden days education used to be the only thing no one could take away from you plan on working three jobs in a riddled time without boobs or the body, I was lucky to get a diploma.

My voice is filled with tintinnabulation sighs of people like Uncle Sol going to his shop every day whistling *I'm Forever Blowing Bubbles* dreams come from prayer shawls the big let down on the other side of the cow shed the American Dream is about making it big cutting out coupons Goldilocks with three bears cooking her instant oatmeal more like the freedom to keep dreaming I will find love pure love easy on the eyes the pocket book a spiritual kind of love makes me go to services say *thank you for this blessing* or talk to a Bay Laurel who listens no matter what the sap rising, dreams are our innocence our incense we burn every night.

Acknowledgments

"Gossip," "In the Shadow of the Middle East," *Bridges: A Jewish Feminist Journal, Vol. 12, Number 2, 2007*

"Leona Canyon," *Canary: Hip Pocket Press, Issue Number 5, 2009*

"The Widow Discovers the Secret of Leona Canyon," *qarrtsiluni, 2011*

"Börte's Perfect Love Song," *Prime Number Magazine, 2011*

"The Last Days Of Genghis Khan," "Manduhai Across The Router," *Conclave A Journal Of Character, 2012*

"How I Went to Jail," *Digital Americana, 2012*

"Two Places," *San Francisco Peace & Hope, 2013*

"Get Your Dervish On," *Poetica Magazine, 2013*

"Seven Things I Will Not Think About in the Last Seconds of My Life," *The Más Tequila Review, 2013*

"In Istanbul, Faith Has No Name," *Radiuslit.org, 2013*

"Xbox Marks the Spot," "Yom Kippur 2005, Yiskor Memorial Service," *Jewerotica, 2013*

"Daughter's GPS Device," *Birmingham Arts Journal, 2014*

"Eastern Tiger Swallowtail," *Twelve Rivers Press, 2014*

About the Artist

Leslie Weissman is an experimental New York-based artist whose interest lies in the exploration of the figure, facial expression, and emotional boundaries. Her work has been on display at The Katonah Museum of Art and the Westchester Center for the Arts. She recently was awarded Special Recognition by Light Space & Time Online Art Gallery for her work *Study 53*. You may view her collection at www.leslieweissman.com.

About the Author

Lenore grew up in New York City, raised a family in the Bay Area, and currently lives in Louisiana. Her work has been widely published in journals and anthologized. Collections include "Tap Dancing on the Silverado Trail" (Finishing Line Press, 2011), "Sh'ma Yis'rael" (Pudding House Publications, 2007), and "Cutting Down the Last Tree on Easter Island" (West End Press, 2012). Her writing has won recognition from Poets & Writers (finalist in California Voices contest) and as a finalist for the Pablo Neruda Prize, Nimrod International Journal. The Society for Technical Communication has recognized her work regarding Technical Literacy in the schools. She edited "From the Well of Living Waters" (Kehilla Community Synagogue, 2011) and serves as the copy editor of *Blue Lyra Review*. Lenore teaches memoir writing in Monroe, Louisiana at the Ouachita Parish Public Library. Her blog resides at www.lenoreweiss.com.